An Accelerated Reader Book

Reading Level: 4.9   Points: 1/2
Disk:

WHY DO WE NEED TO BRUSH OUR TEETH?

BY ISAAC ASIMOV AND CARRIE DIERKS

53095

Gareth Stevens Publishing
MILWAUKEE

For a free color catalog describing Gareth Stevens's list of high-quality children's books, call 1-800-341-3569 (USA) or 1-800-461-9120 (Canada).

The editor would like to thank Dr. Jerome Gildner, D.D.S., of Mequon, Wisconsin, for his assistance with the accuracy of the text and artwork.

The book designer would like to thank Dr. Thomas T. Tang and his staff at Brookfield Family Dentistry, Brookfield, Wisconsin, and the models for their participation. Special thanks to Teri Kraus for the casting and logistics.

Library of Congress Cataloging-in-Publication Data

Asimov, Isaac, 1920-
    Why do we need to brush our teeth? / by Isaac Asimov and Carrie Dierks.
       p. cm. -- (Ask Isaac Asimov)
    Summary: Describes the structure and function of our teeth and the importance of taking care of them.
    Includes bibliographical references and index.
    ISBN 0-8368-0807-X
    1. Teeth--Care and hygiene--Juvenile literature. 2. Dental caries--Prevention--Juvenile literature. [1. Teeth--Care and hygiene.] I. Dierks, Carrie. II. Title. III. Series: Asimov, Isaac, 1920- Ask Isaac Asimov.
    RK63.A78   1993
    617.6'01--dc20   93-20155

Edited, designed, and produced by
Gareth Stevens Publishing
1555 North RiverCenter Drive, Suite 201
Milwaukee, Wisconsin 53212, USA

Picture Credits
pp. 2-3, Paul Miller/Advertising Art Studios, 1993; pp. 4-5, Paul Miller/Advertising Art Studios, 1993; p. 4 (inset), © John Adams/ Adams Picture Library; pp. 6-7, © B. T. Hodgson/Adams Picture Library; p. 7 (inset), © Jeff Robins/Picture Perfect USA; pp. 8-9, Marilyn Hamann/Advertising Art Studios, 1993; p. 8 (inset), © Hans Reinhard/Bruce Coleman Limited; pp. 10-11, Paul Miller/ Advertising Art Studios, 1993; pp. 12-13, Paul Miller/Advertising Art Studios, 1993; pp. 14-15, © SIU/Visuals Unlimited; p. 15 (inset), © E. Masterson/H. Armstrong Roberts; pp. 16-17, © Jay Daniel/Third Coast Stock Source; pp. 18-19, Joanne Bowring, 1993; p. 18 (inset), Paul Miller/Advertising Art Studios, 1993; pp. 20-21, © Bernard Gavin/Adams Picture Library; pp. 22-23, © Jon Allyn, Cr. Photog., 1993; p. 24 © Jon Allyn, Cr. Photog., 1993

Cover photograph, © Jon Allyn, Cr. Photog., 1993: Learning and practicing dental hygiene at an early age can help teeth last a lifetime.

Series editor: Barbara J. Behm
Series designer: Sabine Beaupré
Book designer: Kristi Ludwig
Art coordinator: Karen Knutson
Picture researcher: Diane Laska

Printed in the United States of America

1 2 3 4 5 6 7 8 9 98 97 96 95 94 93

Contents

Words that appear in the glossary are printed in **boldface** type the first time they occur in the text.

Learning about Your Body

The human body is like an amazing machine that can breathe, eat, run, read, play, sleep, and more. Most people usually feel strong and healthy and can carry on these activities without thinking. But like any machine, your body needs care to stay in top working order. For example, you need to take care of your teeth by brushing them. But why is brushing so important? What else can you do to care for your teeth? What happens if you don't? Let's find out.

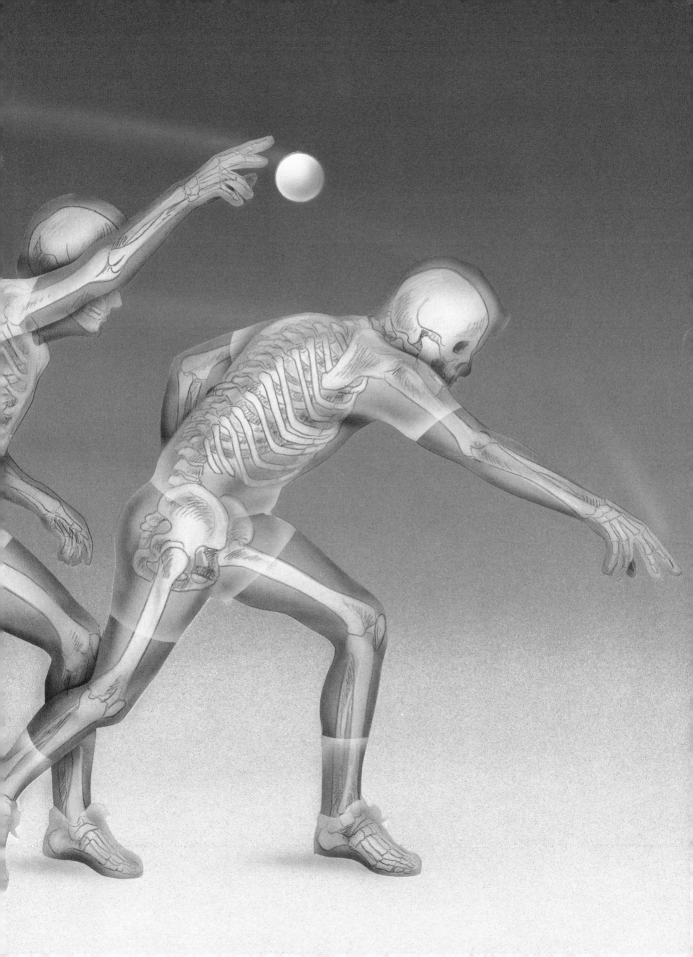

Biting, Chewing, Speaking

How important are your teeth? Without them, you couldn't eat or talk very well! You use your front teeth to tear and bite food. You use your back teeth to chew and grind food. Your teeth also help you form the many sounds necessary for speaking.

Animals use their teeth in many ways, too. Rabbits and rodents use their teeth like tools to gnaw plants and chisel nuts. Wolves and wildcats use their teeth to kill prey for food.

Keeping Teeth Clean

Gnawing on a bone can keep a dog's teeth clean. But *you* have to make a special effort to keep your teeth healthy. Within twenty minutes after eating, the sugars in your food combine with invisible **bacteria** in your mouth to form acids that decay your teeth. Brushing removes bits of food, sugar, and bacteria that remain on your teeth after eating. Flossing removes these substances that have lodged between your teeth.

The Inside Story

To understand tooth decay, you must know
what your teeth are made of. The outside of
a tooth is made of a hard, protective
substance called **enamel**. Under the enamel
is a softer, bony material called **dentin**.

The center of the tooth, or **pulp**, contains
blood vessels and nerves. Blood vessels
carry food and oxygen to the tooth. Nerves
carry messages like "hot!" or "cold!" from
your teeth to your brain. If you get a
toothache, you know something is bothering
a nerve within the pulp.

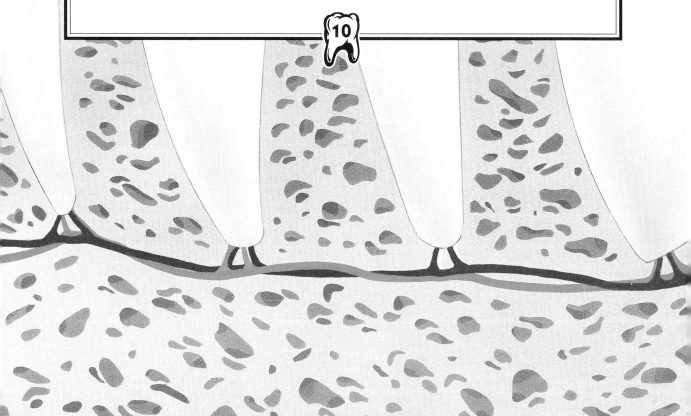

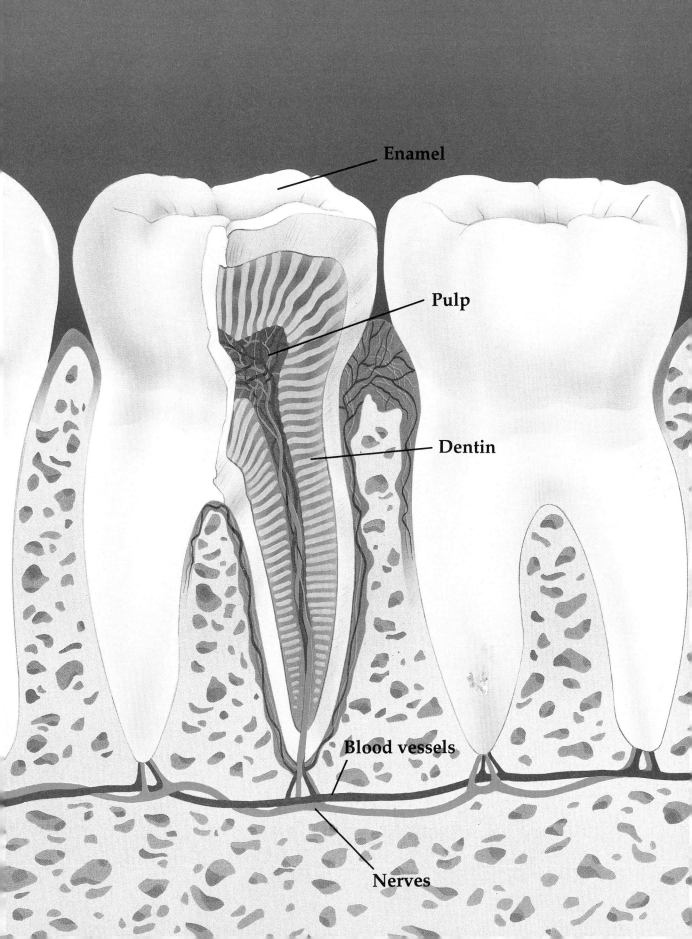

Enamel

Pulp

Dentin

Blood vessels

Nerves

Birth of a Cavity

When sugars combine with bacteria in your mouth, a sticky substance called **plaque** forms on tooth enamel. Brushing your teeth helps remove plaque. But if it continues to build up, acids produced by plaque will eat a

12

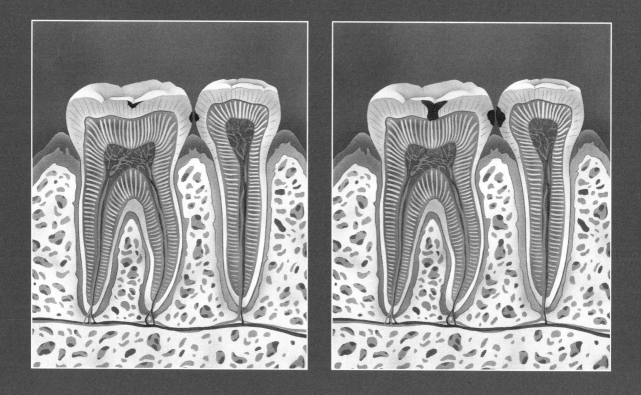

hole, or **cavity**, in the enamel. The cavity has to be treated by a dentist. Left untreated, the cavity may spread into the dentin and then the pulp. If bacteria invade the pulp, the tooth may become infected. The blood vessels swell and press on nearby nerves, causing a painful, throbbing toothache.

13

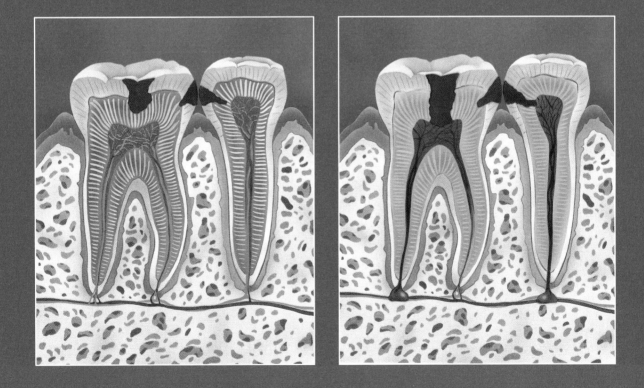

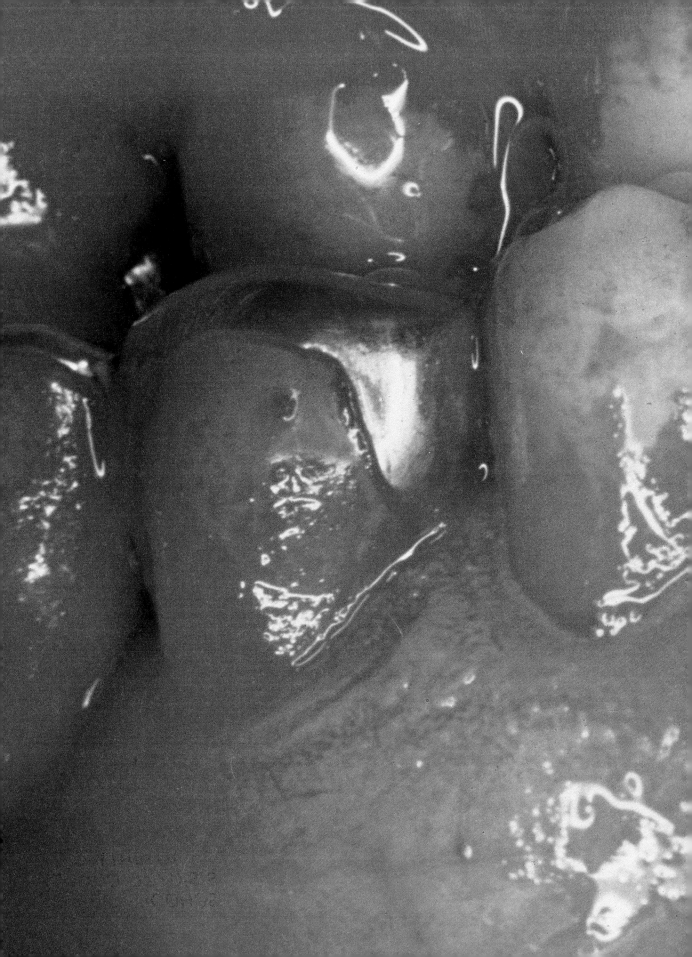

A Mouthful of Trouble

Plaque may eventually harden into a chalky material called **tartar**, which then may cause gum disease. Sometimes, a dentist can treat an infected tooth or diseased gums before permanent damage occurs. But in severe cases, the dentist has no choice but to pull the tooth. If dental problems are left untreated, some people may need to have all their teeth removed.   If this happens, they must wear **dentures**, or false teeth.

Regular visits to the dentist for a check-up and **X rays** are necessary to avoid trouble.

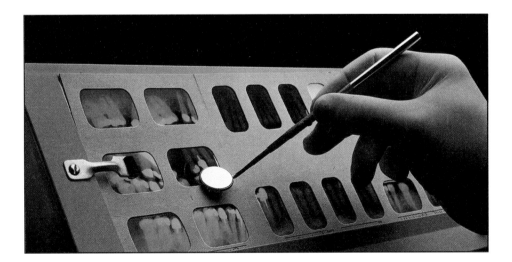

Open Wide!

During your appointment, the dentist will also clean your teeth. He or she will remove any tartar and look for decay or other problems. Regular cleanings every six months are very important. They will help prevent tooth decay and gum disease.

If you do have a cavity, the dentist will remove the decayed part of the tooth and then fill the tooth back in with a strong, protective substance. But don't worry — with a small injection of pain-deadening **anesthetic**, you'll hardly feel a thing!

Brushing Up on Dental Care

Can brushing your teeth really make a difference? Yes, but you must do it right. Brush at least twice a day, especially after eating, using **fluoride** toothpaste. Fluoride is a chemical element that reduces tooth decay. Use a toothbrush with soft, rounded bristles. Brush with short, angled strokes on the front and back sides of your teeth, including the gums. Brush your tongue, too — this will help keep your breath fresh. Flossing removes food and plaque from places your toothbrush cannot reach.

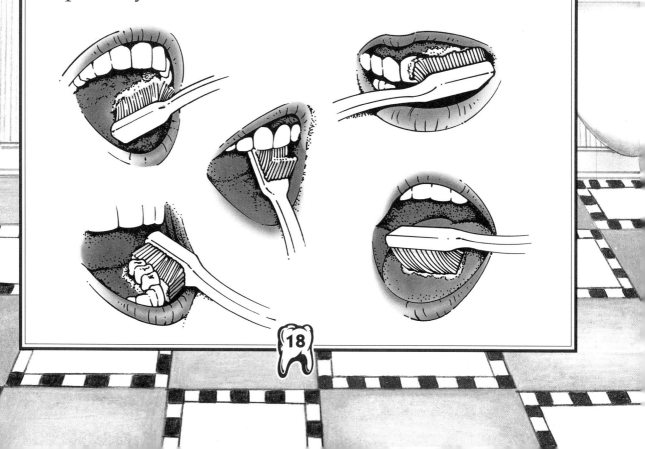

More Food for Thought

Smart eating can go a long way toward keeping teeth healthy.   Many naturally

sweet and starchy foods, like fruit, bread, potatoes, and pasta, are important for a balanced diet.

But your teeth's biggest enemies are sugary snacks like candy, cookies, and sugar-sweetened cereals and soft drinks. Instead of eating these foods, choose smile-saving snacks like plain popcorn, cheese, and nuts.

21

A Smile That Won't Quit

You have probably already begun to lose your baby teeth and to grow adult teeth. These are the last teeth you will have. That's why good dental care is so important now. If you brush and floss your teeth at least twice a day, see your dentist twice a year, and eat wisely, chances are you will enjoy beautiful, healthy teeth throughout your life.

22

More Books to Read

Teeth by John Gaskin (Watts)
The Tooth Book by Alan E. Nourse (McKay)
Your Teeth by Joan Iveson-Iveson (Bookwright Press)

Places to Write

Here are some places you can write for more information about tooth care. Be sure to state exactly what you want to know. Give them your full name and address so they can write back to you.

American Dental Association
211 East Chicago Avenue
Chicago, IL 60611

Canadian Dental Association
1815 Alta Vista Drive
Ottawa, Ontario, KlG 3Y6

Glossary

anesthetic (ănn-ess-THEH-tick): a chemical used in the medical field to deaden feeling in the body.

bacteria (back-TEER-ee-uh): one-celled organisms that live almost everywhere, including the human body.

cavity (CAV-ih-tee): a hole or pit in a tooth.

dentin (DENT-in): the bony middle portion of a tooth.

dentures (DEN-cherz): a set of false teeth.

enamel (ee-NAM-uhl): the hard material making up the outer surface of a tooth.

fluoride (FLURE-ide): a chemical element that prevents tooth decay. It is often added to toothpastes and the water supply.

plaque (PLĂCK): a sticky substance that builds up on the surface of a tooth.

pulp: the soft, inner portion of a tooth that contains nerves and blood vessels.

tartar (TAR-ter): a hard, chalky substance that builds up on teeth when plaque is not removed.

X rays: powerful rays of light that can pass through substances that ordinary rays of light cannot pass through.

Index